I0532435

Turning the Corner

Lori Ulrich

QUILLKEEPERS PRESS

Copyright © Lori Ulrich, 2023
Book Cover Design by Quillkeepers Press
Edit by Dylan Webster and Stephanie Lamb
Format by Quillkeepers Press, LLC

All rights reserved. No part of this book may be reproduced in any form or by any electronic or mechanical means, including information storage and retrieval systems, without the permission in writing from the publisher, except by a reviewer who may quote brief passages in a review.

This compilation contains some works of fiction. Locales and public names are sometimes used for atmospheric purposes. Any resemblance to actual people, living or dead, or to businesses, companies, events, institutions, or locales are completely coincidental. Any references to pop culture are owned by their specific companies and are not the property of the author.

There are some poems here within that represent thoughts of the author. Any resemblance to actual events, locals, or persons, living or dead, is entirely coincidental.

ISBN: 979-8-9868389-9-1

Published by Quillkeepers Press, LLC
PO Box 10236
Casa Grande, AZ 85130

Dedicated to Preston Carter Ulrich

June 8, 1986 – July 3, 2016

Table of Contents

Preston   **9**

I Choose Life, for Love   11

How I Write My Truth   13

I Loved You, My Son   14

Broken   15

One Foot in Front of the Other   17

Tibetan Bowl   18

Vajra   19

After My Son's Passing   20

Sixty-Five Feet Above Sea Level   22

Splayed   25

February 14th   26

The Biggest Lie I Ever Told   27

Heaven's Halo   29

Tibetan Prayer   30

Every Line Sings Your Memory   **31**

Because…
Every Line Sings Your Memory, My Son   33

On a Stormy July Evening   34

Yesterday Will Never Be Here   36

When Jesus Came   37

One of a Kind (not the cliché) 38

Conversations at 2:00 am. 40

Moons Ago 42

Color of Bones 43

I Dream Away 44

Fly Away, Anywhere but Here 45

Heart Roses 46

Rodriquez Has Left Me to Wonder… 47

Thanks for Your Time 49

Coffee and a Chat 51

A Different Kind of Vision 52

Live Your Loving Life 54

Thirteen Journals 56

Season's Pass **57**

Prairie Roads 59

When Loneliness Comes 60

Nothing is Predictable Now 61

Cloud Cover Leaves No Room for Blue Sky 62

Seasons Pass 63

A Good Snowfall 64

Snowshoeing in the Afternoon 65

Winter Morning 67

Snow Globe 68

Cozy 69

New Socks 70

Losing Ground 71

Homecoming 72

Reading is a Gateway 73

Just Saying 74

Stone Angel 75

Treading Water 76

Lake Therapy 77

Six Years 78

Early Riser 79

Dear Robert Frost 80

Rose Quartz 81

Good Morning, Sunshine 82

Acknowledgements **83**

About the Author **85**

Preston

I Choose Life, for Love

I wake distraught, reach for
my husband's hand, his warmth.

His touch tethers me
keeps me grounded

when I dream of dying
when my body starts to lift

when anxiety comes for me
in the dark, when I sleep.

Preston was nine when he was
diagnosed with a brain tumor.
Sixty percent chance of survival.
Three years of chemotherapy.
He went blind.

Aggressive brain cancer.
No chance of survival.
Alternative treatments.
Hospice at our home.
He died at thirty.
Loved by his wife, family, friends.

I fear my spirit being taken
against my will.

Is heaven a place for those
who carry too much pain?

Memories torture me. My mind
relives each moment of his struggle.

Eyes open, I fear what I'd do
without my husband.

Would I also rise, leave
my earth body behind?

How I Write My Truth

his name
holds itself on my tongue
after four years I still
can't say it without tears
a break in my voice

my son's door was always open
welcomed with a cup of his favorite coffee
homemade chocolate chip cookies
he gave me his best chair, his only chair
listened, without judgement

his words have stayed with me
I never left his home without a hug
I look at his picture, whisper

can you hear me
do you know I can't say it

I can't say your name.

I Loved You, My Son

I am ok for awhile
to the point where I wonder why.

Then it hits.
A dose of reality.

Sleepless nights.
Memories, last months of life.

I don't need reminding.
I was there.

I loved you, my son.
I am not ok.

I wish it were
different.

So many dreams
left with you.

Broken

I am   broken.
My son lost his life to brain cancer.
I am   broken—

a ripe melon
splattered against a wall
insides oozing out.

Why is there always pressure
to explain broken?
I am   broken
means chest pain, anxious,
irregular heartbeat, faint.

Lying awake at night
my heart pounds
with intense pain. I wonder
if it will explode.

Shortness of breath
catches up to me in the daytime—
I stop, stand still, hyperventilate
tell myself I will be ok.

I am   broken.

My son lost his life to brain cancer.
I am   broken.

I read the Dali Lama, Buddhist teachings,
psalms from the Bible, follow
the Indigenous Medicine Wheel,
try guided meditation, learn Reiki,
hope to settle my shattered spirit.

I wish to wrap my heart in a soft cloth,
place it in a bottom dresser drawer.

Rest my darling.

I am   broken.
My son lost his life to brain cancer.
I am   broken.

One Foot in Front of the Other

Soul music plays
in my head. A bass drum vibrates,
my heart throbs.

How did I get here?
There appears to be
no way out.

I take step after step in spiral form,
arrive at the center, see a large painted rock.
I've no idea what it means. There is no one to ask.

I sit by the stone, trace its cracks,
deep fissures. I too am cracked like this,
jagged, faded.

I walk backwards, rewind. Soul music's
steady beat pushes against my chest.
Step back.   Step back.   Step   back.

Tibetan Bowl

A Tibetan singing bowl rests on a memory shelf
beside Preston's picture, a Tibetan gong, vajra,
small carved piece of cherrywood and braided sweetgrass.

The bowl fits in the palm of my hand. I bought it as a gift
for him in a retro-shop, full of nostalgia. It was on a table
with carved stone Buddhas, incense sticks,
chakra stones and essential oils.
I played the meditation bell,
listened to its voice.

I remember his surprise.
Without vision, there were things
he knew only by touch. He ran
his fingers around the rim
marveled at its smoothness.

He circled the mallet clockwise around the outer edge
in a slow, repetitive motion.
Sitting cross-legged on the floor
he cupped the bowl in his hand.
It vibrated, played with prolonged energy.
His body relaxed. He smiled.

I close my eyes, hold the singing bowl in my palm,
imagine his strong steady hand over mine,
run the mallet around, around, around—

Vajra

The vajra came home in a box
after my son's death, along with
his Tibetan sound bowl, Tingsha bells
and lotus shaped incense burner.

Deep in heartache, I placed the vajra
on a shelf, where it sat for years.
Unsure of its meaning or use I paid it
little attention.

A few years later, I saw
a vajra on display in a store.
Later, I read of its purpose.

In the center of the bronze vajra is a sphere. A lotus
emerges on each side, one symbolizes the
physical world, one represents an enlightened
state of reality. Each lotus folds itself in,
points touch in the shape of a cross.

Preston was a man of few possessions.
A seeker of spiritual power, he meditated
to focus his mind. He welcomed religions
of the world into his heart.

I roll my son's vajra between my fingers, pray,
his wisdom at rest, in the palm
of my hand.

After My Son's Passing

I settle in the music room, created for comfort.
The walls have inspirational quotes
by John Lennon and Bob Marley,

posters of Jimi Hendrix, Janis Joplin, The Beatles.
There is a picture of my grandson, playing my son's drums.
The CD case has over three hundred selections of his music.

A wooden bookshelf houses my son's Tibetan sound
bowl, vajra, a whittled piece of cherry wood, incense
burner with cones of sage, amber, rose and
frankincense, a box of instruments, a mouth harp,
harmonica, wooden and metal flutes, a native deer hide
hand drum. There is one picture of him, holding his
nephew and smiling.

In one corner of the room there is a rocking chair, a basket
with my journals, writing in stages, poems finished
and unfinished, an assortment of poetry books,
magazines, Chakra healing and Buddha teachings.
Beside the chair is a small table, draped with a seven-chakra
tapestry. A small Buddha sits in the center of the table,
along with my own bronze Tibetan bowl, a book on
angels, a psalm book of prayers, salt lamp and a cup
with an assortment of pens and pencils.

My husband plays his guitar here in the early morning,
throughout the day, and at night.

Self-taught he has built a strong song repertoire; his
daily strumming soothes and heals.

I sit in the center of the room, light a Zen candle, turn
whispers of words into poetry,
meditate, ground myself, breathe.
Wind blows in through an open window.
Tibetan bells chime.

Sixty-Five Feet Above Sea Level

I pack the usual for Mexico, bathing suits, light dresses,
shorts, tank tops, hat, sandals, sturdy runners for walking.
My backpack also holds a small box filled with a handful
of my son's ashes.
My husband and I never know where we will disperse
them, trust the right place will find us. On our travels
the past few years
we've scattered them in waterfalls, quiet prairies, canyons,
and open seas coast to coast.

My husband and I take a ferry from Cancun to Isle Mujeres.
We rent a golf cart to tour around the island. Punta Sur offers
the ruins of Ixchel Temple. We pay thirty pesos at the entrance
to walk the curved paths to the sea. Mayan artwork
is positioned along the way, metal signs describe the artist
and year of the sculptures. We stop to read each one.
Iguanas bask on the rocks, seagulls dip down in search
of food, sea turtles swim freely in their sanctuary.

The ruins rest on the edge of a cliff.
Ancient Mayan built their temple facing bright sun,
honoring the Mayan Goddess of the moon, fertility, and love.
Walking on the path carved thousands of years before,
we sense the company of our son in the heat of the
afternoon. We descend the stone steps closer to the

turquoise sea, feel the breeze and ocean spray. Sounds of
water wash onto rocks, roar in our ears.

A small plaque screwed into the rocks reads,
Cliff of the Dawn. Welcome those who look to be
the first ones kissed by the sun.
Our son swam on Mexican beaches several years ago.
A Shaman read his palm; told him he had no lifeline.
He told him he was angel.
With a catch in his throat, our son shared this story with us.
Four short years later he died from brain cancer.

The path, wet from the splash of sea, becomes unstable.
We slow down, grip the handrail, go up the stone staircase
to the peak. Wings beat in air.
Waves crash on jagged rocks below.
 Mist rises, the sea froths.
Wild waves roll with music.
On the wind, from the water below, we hear him.

This is the place.
Two security guards sit around the corner, backs towards us.

We find a crevasse in the ruins of Ixchel Temple, with full sun,
protected from wind and water. We block their view
with our bodies, carve out a small hole in the fine
rubble, bury his ashes,
cover them with loose stones.
Faces to the sea, salt mist dampens our cheeks.

Previously published in the Saskatchewan Writers Guild,
Emerging Saskatchewan Writers
Spring Magazine, Vol. 13. 2022.

Splayed

Words disrobe, slip
into something uncomfortable,
make the reader cringe.

Naked
on a white page.

Between each word
is a space.
Whiteness speaks
to all the things
I cannot.

February 14th

I write in my journal, grip
my pen. Tears slide down
my cheeks, smear words.

A small flame flickers, twists and turns
disturbed. It licks the insides
of my Himalayan Salt candle holder.

Scented rose votive melts.
I inhale slowly. Exhale.
Remind myself to keep breathing.

The heat of my words
places the loss of you on paper. There is
no denying them.

I am all my words, and none of them.
With shaky hands and damp eyes, I write.
It is the only thing I know.

The Biggest Lie I Ever Told

When it became clear
that you would die soon
I tried to say it all.

I told you I loved you, over
and over, day after day,
so you'd know.

I told you I was proud of you,
of the confident young man
you'd become.

I told you your positive spirit
and energy flowed into the hearts
of those who knew you well.

I told you I was elated you'd
found someone to love as deeply
as you did, someone you'd marry.

I told you I'd never trade the journey
you took your dad and I on throughout
your life for anything.

I told you I'd be ok, we'd be ok,
we'd look after each other,
it was ok for you to go.

I'd read this was what a person was supposed
to do, set their loved one free,
to help them on their journey.

I've regretted those words ever since.
I'm not ok. We're not ok.
Not without you. I lied.

Years later I sit with memories,
wonder how I could have been
so naïve.

How am I supposed
to keep breathing when
you are no longer here.

Heaven's Halo

I sit in lamplight
watch shadows circle the wall.

Nestled in a green recliner, wrapped
in a blanket shawl, I write.

My mind travels backwards to the places
I have already been.

The sudden diagnosis, alternative
cancer treatments, hospice at home.

I sip on cinnamon tea
rewrite my son's history.

Days turn into months
turn into years.

I write, rewrite, edit.
I write until I believe my words.

Until it is an ending
I can live with.

Tibetan Prayer

A light breeze tickles my ears
blows wisps of hair over my eyes.

I tread water. Small ripples wave outward.
I extend my arms in heart shaped motions,
paddle the length of the pool.

I come here to pray.
The clouds slight blue hue
matches the water.

I float, hear my heartbeat. Stillness
gives way to meditation.

I press my palms together,
thumbs rest light
against my chest.

A Buddhist greeting to my son
who swims in the heavens.

Every Line Sings Your Memory

Because...
Every Line Sings Your Memory, My Son

Musicians invite me in
with their song, offer
me words to hold
when my heart is breaking.

Only the good die young, sings Billy Joel.
I shed tears every time I hear this song.
You were good. You were young.
You had living left to do.

Leonard Cohen's famous song, *Anthem*
speaks of hope in the darkness.
Waiting for that sliver of light
keeps me going.

Pictures of you
throughout the house.

Every time I see your picture,
sings Luba. I shed tears when I walk past
your wedding photograph.

Bob Dylan's *Forever Young*
cuts deep. I never hear the end
of the song. You didn't have the chance
to grow older. You remain—forever young.

On a Stormy July Evening

Sky cracked.
Thunder boomed.
God called,
Come up to my house.

Drums of thunder
walked my son home.
Heaven's music welcomed him
with rushing wind, rumbling
and lightning. The sky opened,
rain fell.

He didn't go easily.
Surrendering was not his nature.
On a stormy early July evening
he fought for life, for love.
High winds blew in from an open
bedroom window.
Angels whispered -

Come, I will take your pain

My son reached out with his hand.

He loved life, lived every moment.
Even in dark times
he found joy.

On stormy nights I search
for the crack in sky
flash of light.
I know my son is not far away.
Someday, he will call—

Come up to my house.

Yesterday Will Never Be Here

The night my son died the sky filled
with black clouds, raging wind
thunder and lightning. Moon shone
in the aftermath. Air turned silent.

My son is not coming back.
Yesterday will never be here.

I see the road before me
follow it to where
I walk alone.
I say good-bye.

Yesterday will never be here.

I imagine him saying—

*Keep walking and I will be with you
in the crimson heart of the moon.*

The moon casts a shadow.
Tonight's solar eclipse turns
from gray to orange to a deep shade
of red before my eyes.

Yesterday will never be here.

When Jesus Came

My son's story
ended too soon.

The second time cancer came for him
Preston said it was a lesson, to teach him to be kinder,
more understanding, more loving.
He taught the rest of us how to fight for life,
live for love.

He never asked for sympathy.
He walked his own path,
carried a zest for life,
lived full throttle.
Known for his welcoming nature
he gathered a following.

When Jesus came for him,
the night the horizon came alive,
thunder cracked the sky open.
There was music.

My son left this earth
a better place.

One of a Kind (not the cliché)

Don't say goodbye.
Think of me as
background bass
in your favorite song.

Listen to my lyrics,
I sent you a message.
Can you hear me
call out for justice?

I play for the marginalized society
in underground music venues.
Rise up with my words.
Act.

Be your own show.
Self-define.

Used to hold back.
Now I want it all.

Every single dream starts in the mind.
Living large in the stars, one of a kind.

Every time there is inequity
and people gather, I am there
in the center of the crowd
calling for change.

Don't say goodbye.
I am the voice in your heart, saying,
The world needs you to speak up.

Conversations at 2:00 am.

Buds on Broadway
has a back door
where patrons step out
for a joint in the alley.

A professor who listens to the blues
discusses the flailing economy
with the Hell's Angel while the band's
on a break. Intellectuals talk with writers
about the lack of political transparency.
Street people say jobs are hard to come by.

They all speak of friends
who have died.

Preston's ghost stands beside them, hears
his name, catches a whiff of rising smoke.

I imagine he's smiling, laughing even.
He always played devil's advocate.

I play my own game. When you don't
fit in with the mainstream you've got
two choices, tune out and drop out, or stand up.
Justice happens outside of the rules.

The last man nods,
shuffles off towards home.
Preston's ghost departs.

Early dawn sprinkles diamond
patterns on parked cars.
Dewdrops wink
in morning light.

Moons Ago

Moon calls.
Its crescent shape
a bowl to catch star dust.

A far-off piano melody
welcomes me into
nighttime song.

Lunar's changing face measures
many moons
my son has been gone.

Hammock of waning moon
carried him off to dark skies
filled with silver stars.

Every night I stand outside,
search the heavens,
listen for his song, pray.

The moon wanes.
A bright star winks.
My heart softens.

Color of Bones

A vacancy sign hangs in the window
of my eyes.
I keep the music room neat, dust occasionally,
organize, reorganize, keep busy.
Treasures tucked away in boxes,
a few displayed on a shelf—
Tibetan sound bowl, gong, vajra,
cherrywood carving and a
braid of sweetgrass.
My son smiles in his picture.

When he left his earth home
part of me went with him.
I lay down, pain blankets me.
I draw covers over my head.
Stop breathing.

I am gone. No one knows.

My eyes are full moons, color of bones.
They search every night—

for something he might have left behind
something he will return for.

I Dream Away

In the flutter of lashes
behind closed eyes

I dream away
tears

dream away
goodbyes

dream away
yesterdays

nothing is wrong
cancer didn't happen

you remain
young, strong

I dream away
gray skies

find a place where
the sun always shines

a time when your smile and
infectious laughter lit up the room

I close my eyes, hear your music
dream away

Fly Away, Anywhere but Here

Wind flattens grasses, branches snap off trees,
tumbleweeds reel across fields, swirling dust
obscures the sky.

String lights blow off the deck roof,
bulbs crack.

I once sat in the red chair
now upside-down in the yard.

There is no place for me here—

My body's in the prairies
but my heart is with you.

I follow the lift of geese, fly with them
to where heartbreak never happened

where sky is quiet, blue.
Clouds morph from the face of a child
to a soft swaying hammock.

Geese settle by a slow river,
gather in reeds along shore
warmed by sun.

I rise, with tilted wings.

Heart Roses

I wear a red rose on my left forearm,
tattooed petals that never fade.
Experience Connection handwritten
in black ink beside it. My son's traced initials
complete the tattoo.

Every year in late spring I buy miniature roses
for my kitchen table.
I should be used to carrying on without him.
It has been five years.

Summer's exit always leaves a tear.
Rose petals wilt and drop,
signs of fall, a need for warmer clothing.
Winter's entrance hurts.

Red was my son's favorite color.

I expected to sit with him
on a park bench
in every season, every year
of my life.

Rodriquez Has Left Me to Wonder...

I wonder about how I can reclaim the empty space
in my heart, live with lonely.

I wonder about death and its permanency. Every day
I pick up my pen. All words speak of my son.

I wonder about forgiveness for the woman
who asked me if I had other children when my son
died. She replied, "It's ok. You still have *one.*"

I wonder if I will ever sleep without fear.

I wonder about our world and can it be saved.

I wonder about disease, hatred, violence
and racism.

And I wonder about the tear in my daughter's eye,
my grandson's questions about Uncle Preston and Heaven.

I wonder what would happen if time rewound
and our loved ones were granted another chance.

I wonder if we truly listen to the stories of others
if we'll meet a friend.

I wonder about others who live as I do
in a state of panic. Watchful. Waiting.

And I wonder when a cure for cancer will be found.

I wonder why every time I turn to walk away the road curves,
leads me back to love.

I wonder, I wonder if I will ever stop wondering.

Thanks for Your Time

Doors close to those with a disability.
Most people don't see past the obvious.

Your blindness is a liability. You can't see the clients
you'd be working with, employers told my son
when he looked for a job after earning his degree
in Sociology: Crime and Justice.

"Thanks for your time," Preston said.

He tried other doors, diversified his options,
took more courses, researched his interests,
volunteered.

He'd say, "It's ok. I'll find a way."

Doors closed on him
for years.

His persistence grew, an unwillingness
to give in to the opinions of men and women
who judged his abilities.

Preston created a room he could
open and close, with tools
for his massage therapy practise,
a table, towels, reflexology chair, essential oils.

He framed his degrees and diplomas,
hung them on the wall.

He'd smile, open the door
for his clients to come in.
"Thanks for your time," he'd say.

Coffee and a Chat

"Come in," my son would call when I knocked on his
door for a visit.
"I made a fresh pot of coffee; would you like a cup?
How about a cookie? I made them with spelt flour and
carob chips."

Our conversations were always long. We spoke of anything
and everything. My favorite topics were his views on politics
and religion. Never a dull moment.

He'd tell me his friends told him, "You're not like the rest."

He'd add, "Friends trust me with their struggles. I listen.
Tell them where it's at."

He'd laugh, "Who's perfect anyway?
Look at me, all the shit I've done!"

He'd say, "I give them a cup of coffee. Just sit. Give them
space to talk. I keep their secrets. That's why
they keep coming back."

When I left his apartment, we'd hug. Often as I
walked down the stairs I'd pass one of his friends
on their way up.

A Different Kind of Vision

No one expected him
to be so eloquent in his speech
be direct, call them out—

injustices witnessed, housing for the poor,
disabled rights, political inequities.
Being blind, he'd say, gave him an edge.
He had vision, saw things in a unique way.

"Being blind makes you a liability," he was told
applying for jobs. "A danger to the clients and yourself."

He walked the streets. Saw how the homeless really live.
Stopped to chat. Put a loonie in a busker's guitar case,
listened to the beat poet.

He'd seek out employment wherever he could. He had
a degree, experience. Employers wavered, hesitant
to take a chance.

He'd make appointments at the offices of Members of
Parliament.
He was met with misgivings.

Word on the street.
They don't know what's happening
outside their office door.

I am here. Ready.
To listen. Take a stand.

Who's the blind guy now?

Live Your Loving Life

Preston was twenty when he pinned a black and white poster
of Janis Joplin on his bedroom wall. All she wore
on her body were strands of long beaded necklaces
with four bangle bracelets on her left hand.
Her long wavy hair almost covering her face.
She looked pensive; her piercing eyes followed the viewer.
At the bottom of the poster, in bold ink
1943-1970.

His friends teased about a blind guy's attraction
to a naked girl's picture. His friend David laughed, stuck
push pins in her nipples so Preston could get a feel for them.
Janis was one of his favorite vocalists.
Her full, rich tone in,
"As Good as You've Been to This World,"
reminds me of his love for living.

The lyrics speak of karma.
Have good intentions.
Treat others well.
What you give the world
will come back to you.
Live the best you can—

And he did.

Last evening, more than five years
after his death, his friend Char told me
she misses him.
He was a good friend, there aren't many
people like that around. She reminisced
about the good times they had.

They met at a summer camp for visually impaired
when they were ten. Stayed in touch for twenty years.
She told me how every year he'd make everyone
at camp laugh, leave his cabin late at night, prank people,
scrape his fingers down window screens and make
animal noises. Scare them all silly!

At home, I look at his Janis Joplin poster
now pinned up in our music room.
I play her CD, listen to the lyrics,
"As Good as You've Been to This World."
Tears stream down. I hold a black and white photo
of Preston in my hands.
1986-2016.

Thirteen Journals

Six years. Thirteen journals.
I write every day
to keep my son's spirit close.

Time passes—

through days, months, and years,
through holidays and birthdays,
through family milestones,
his nephew's first birthday, the
birth of his niece who carries his
middle name, the passing of his
beloved grandmother,
through every season,
through sunrises and sunsets,
through light and darkness.
Through all of these
he has been gone.

If I could turn back time.

I'd bring him back.
I'd cure his cancer, twice.
I'd return his sense of sight.

If I could turn back time.

Season's Pass

Prairie Roads

I bike down prairie paths by my home
hear gravel grind under my tires.
I watch for larger stones, swerve,
continue, with a slow turn of pedals.

Leaves on poplar, willow
and maple color the fields.
Golden amber, burnt orange
dappled green and crimson shine
brilliant against straw pastures
and blue sky. Occasional
flocks of geese ruffle the air.

Every day I bike the same roads
ride over the same stones.
Leaves fall, cool wind blows.
The honk of geese call
my eyes upward. I hear
their powerful wings.

The geese will return in spring
as new buds blossom on poplar.
But you won't.

When Loneliness Comes

I rock on my bench swing,
stare out at the patchwork of neighboring fields.
Fall colors blend—
golden yellow, rust orange, mute brown.
I notice how orderly they appear.

A bull elk`s deep throated bugle
slices the air with confidence.
Brown grasses bend in wind`s direction.
Their flexibility and grace light as a dancer
bowing to their partner.

A squawking magpie sends
tiny chickadees flitting to shelter
in a scotch pine. The black and white tyrant
takes ownership of the birdseed
I put out yesterday.

Anger rises in my chest. I let it out with a scream
that chases away the great-horned owl
who greeted me every day in summer
and into fall. Even the magpie raises its head
in alarm.

Nothing is Predictable Now

Freshly washed indigo blue sheets
hang on the clothesline to dry.
Bedding bends, dances in delight
a slow waltz in early morning.

There is every reason to believe
this is going to be a good day.

The weather station failed to predict
sudden ninety km. gale force winds.
Gusts toss my sheets
high over the clothesline
back down, turning and twisting them
into a messy knot.

I run from the house.
Hair blows across my face.
Forceful winds push me sideways.
I run to the line, unclasp pins
hold tight to each sheet
manage to wrestle them
to the ground.

Cloud Cover Leaves No Room for Blue Sky

I sit in a wicker chair in my glass
sunroom. The rain starts to fall,
a light sprinkle. There is no wind
to alter its direction.

Musty dirt, thick and
pungent sharpen my senses.
Scented pine needles, marigolds
in planter beds, poplar and willows.

The rain picks up speed,
splashes on the windows.
Clouds swell, sway heavy,
release.

Seasons Pass

The sun stretches, takes longer
to rise in September.

There is no hurry. Steam rises
from my coffee mug, reminds me
of incense, escaping into clouds.

The fog lifts, light shines on the
golden fields. They are ready
for harvest.

It is cooler outside. Leaves change
from deep green to pale yellow.
I need to find my plaid jacket.

I take a fall walk by the river,
come home, make fresh garden soup.
I cut green beans, beets, onions and
tomatoes. The beets color my fingers red.

A Good Snowfall

nature hears
stillness
in snowfall

each tiny snowflake
intricate
one of a kind

hope sparkles
glistens in
midday sun

kindness of snow
covers the most
unsightly

unspoken thoughts
come and go
fleeting in time

a good snowfall is deep
sinks into the soul
goes to sleep in the mind

Snowshoeing in the Afternoon

I align my snowshoe poles,
move them in rhythm.
Right foot, left pole. Left foot, right pole.
I stop, set my start. I am not
a natural at winter sports.

Today's venture offers bold sun.
Squinting in the brightness of the coldly white
and opaque deep powder, I marvel at snow sparkle.
One foot, and then the other.
The snow crunches under my feet.
My ski poles punch out cookie-cutter holes
as I mark out my path.
I walk towards the horizon, step out of solid
firm footing, up into beckoning sky.

Snowshoeing through a hazy mist
the view is not what I expected.
There is nothing here, no clear direction.

Right foot, right pole. Left foot, left pole.
My rhythm is broken. Without the weight of earth
there is no indentation marking my presence,
no looking back to see how far I have come, where I
stopped to rest, drew hearts in the snow, where I sat
down to admire the view, where I challenged myself
to keep going.

I walk for a while, unsure of my footing
until I see a thin line of separation
through the fog, not too far off.
I walk slowly towards home,
a grounding I understand.

Winter Morning

I turn cold
when I can't remember
how to stand in the light.

I am outside without a coat.
Snow cast on spruce and
jack pine covers their bareness.

Winter white.
The only footprints are
those of a lone coyote.

I shiver. Deep within
a guttural cry
escapes.

Snow Globe

I shake the snow globe.
Flakes swirl round and round in circles.
Within the dome, the scene remains unchanged. Painted
lips never fade. People never leave.

Rosy cheeked children wear knitted hats and scarves,
coats to their knees. They build a snowman, skate on a
round mirror, are pulled on a wooden toboggan up a
small hill. Couples hold hands out on an evening stroll.
Ladies in a horse-drawn carriage stop to chat with a girl
on the street. She wears a fur cape, a muff encircles her
hands. Her tiny red lips painted into a smile.

An elegant Victorian home shines brightly at night. A
homemade wreath adorns the door. A Christmas tree,
decorated with dried fruit, cookies, nuts, and strands of
cranberries stands in a window. Snow sparkles on the
boughs of evergreens outside.

I shake down a blizzard, with both hands. I shake and
shake and shake.

Smiles do fade. People do leave.

I slam the snow globe on the table. Glass cracks.

Cozy

I peel off worry layers
sink naked into my flannel sheets
cozy in for the night.

I count my breaths.
Inhale, exhale.
Leave the day behind.

Soft scented lavender stones
rest in a bowl
on my bedside table.

I listen to night sounds
ticking cuckoo clock, furnace
hum, sighing water pipes.

New Socks

This morning I'm wearing a pair
of fuzzy ankle socks with grip soles.
In my bottom dresser drawer
there are four pairs of these socks
still in their plastic wrappers.
I've been saving them for years,
no idea why.

Cross-legged on the couch, I trace my fingers
over my socks, outline the zigzag pink, yellow
and blue pattern. I'm reading Patrick Lane's, *Winter*.
Wind blows without remorse.

I read this as wind rattles windows
snow skirmishes through trees and across the fields.
Fog gray sky blends low to touch the earth, like
the thickest socks on a chilly day.

All this whiteness is an open journal.
I write with Patrick Lane.

Losing Ground

I look down walking on icy sidewalks
navigate each step. I go around puddles
covered by a thin layer of verglas. When
I was a child I would stomp on ice
with my boots, stand and let dirty water
rise around me. Now, I tread widely
to the outside, place one foot down
at a time in crunchy snow, too afraid to fall.

Today on my walk there is sleet, it
stings my face. I am determined
to keep my routine route, it calms
the worries I carry. I remove my hat.
Freezing rain falls on my scalp,
drips down my cheeks.

Sometimes I slip, lose my grounding.
Ice pockets on the sidewalk crack
when they're stepped on. Fractured
lifelines break. It reminds me of how quickly
things can change. In the instant it takes
for my boot to fill with water I am back
to childhood days, when getting wet meant getting
up and getting on with living.

Homecoming

My favorite hot apple cider sits on a table
in my sunroom. My view through the large
glass windows is wide open to the farm waking up
in early spring. I have a front row seat. I sit by
the electric fireplace, a beige blanket on my lap.

A chickadee flits branch to branch amongst the caragana.
It carries small sticks and dry grass into a vacant
birdhouse. I admire its resilience. Fingers of sunlight
warm its wings. Thankful birdsong, this small chickadee
enjoys its moments.

Snow melt in the fields seeps into
awakening soil. The prairies are patchy, a mix
of snow and exposed pasture. Black dirt puddles.
On this near windless day, a small bird
lines its home, prepares for nesting.

Today I see winter's impermanence, and
the confidence of a chickadee, at rest in
bare tree branches, a silhouette against
clear blue sky.

Reading is a Gateway

I borrowed a novel from the library. I read
in my sunroom, sun warm on my back. I'm
an observer, perhaps a friend of the main character.
We have both lost someone we love, she her best friend
and me, my son.

Emma confuses reality with the dreams
she lives in, a multi-dimension universe.
I transport into her narrative for a few days, watch her
life unfold. I delve into the plot, examine
characters, know her pain. Think about my own.

I am hungry for story. A wild mind knows when
it needs to be occupied. Hours go by. I stay
seated, resist the urge to bolt. I read
to make sense of what happened here,
six years ago, in spring.

Just Saying

What would happen if I just lay
here on the ground?

Would birds walk on me,
not knowing I was someone?

Would the wind come in waves, spread
a leaf blanket?

Would tall grasses grow through
my body? Would I become an anchor for roots?

Would the rain land first in droplets
or pour itself into my open mouth?

What if I called out in a low moan
like a wounded prairie doe?

Would you come? Would you come
and look for me?

Stone Angel

A small, red jasper angel lay in a display box with other
carvings. Its luster draws me towards it. I pick it up,
feel an energy surge, my left palm tingles.
Is this angel the one—

with tall wings and folded prayer hands. Elegant. Simple.
A chalcedony mineral, with a smooth finish.

I had a dream, just before Christmas.
Its message urgent. I was to find and purchase
an angel in remembrance of my son. I woke restless.
He'd have no interest in a blonde, ringlet haired
porcelain faced doll.

Four months later, at a Rock and Gem Show
this red root chakra angel chose me.

I place it on the windowsill in my study. When the sun
streams in, my angel warms.

I rub its polished wings with the tips
of my fingers. The flutter in my heart lessens.
I begin to write.

Treading Water

I tread water
arms just under the surface.
Legs circle, slow and steady.
Water ripples, remains silent.

I breathe, think about
what is
what was
what could have been—

Wind whispers in the willows.
I can't make out their words.
The earth smells musty, moist
after fresh rain. Summer roses
open their petals.

Restless spirits of my ancestors
walk in clouds, their footsteps
thunder a chorus.
I swim to the edge.

Clouds shift, change.
They never pose
for the same photo twice.
Billowy white, they stretch
into something dangerous—

Wind rises.
Sky darkens.

Lake Therapy

the chilly northern lake beckons
if you want your story, come in and get it

I walk over rough rocks
jagged edges sharp under my tender feet

I walk in deeper
towards fine sand

deeper, to where the lake bottom turns
to soft mud

slow walking meditation
impermanent footprints below water

waves rock in rhythm
threaten to tip my body backward

I walk further
cold shock exhilarates

my body fills with words
I carry them back to shore

let their story
spill

Six Years

My pen is still, thoughts are few.
I sit in my sunroom, look out the large windows,
see the same blue spruce and poplar I did yesterday.
A sparrow family flies in and out of the birdhouse
that faces this room. Air wafts through the screens,
scents of pine, wild roses, ripening blueberries,
garden greens.

There is slight change from yesterday. Except yesterday
tightened my breath. Six years since Preston died. Six years.
I ache —all over.

I twirl my pen around in my fingers, around
and around. A wasp spins at the window.
Flies trapped between screen and glass.
I hear the familiar call of the great-horned owl
who lives in our yard. My dog barks.
I read poems. Can't find one I like.

I flip back the pages of my journals, the ones I've written
in every day since he died. I turn the pages back, back,
further back, until the day darkens
and stars dot the sky.

Early Riser

I wake to cobalt sky. I yearn to fold myself
in its darkness, lay in morning's awakening.
Clouds pillow in white softness.

Later, they stretch themselves into a thin blanket
of pale slate. Behind gray lies a blue
so blue it stays with me throughout my day.

Part the thin veil, remember mornings,
the gift of new beginnings. There is more
beyond what the eye can see.

Sadness is not fostered by the color of sky,
but by unwillingness to see through gray,
relax in blue memories.

Dear Robert Frost

I fled deep into the woods where the trail ends,
pushed further, disappeared, after my son's
terminal brain cancer diagnosis.

I walk in the forest, tread on leaves
give them their first footprint,
bend branches with my hands.
Tangled brambles lead me in circles.
I emerge in the same clearing I walked
through earlier.

The road less traveled
isn't a road.

I walked this path for years.

I can't dispute the unmarked, wild beauty
here. Tall pines reach up for a sky embrace,
sun shines through aspen boughs, nurtures
the forest floor. Breaks in the woods open
to meadows and small tear-shaped ponds.

Robert, I've been in the woods a long time
and it has made a difference.
I stand on a path leading home, my arms
laden with journals.

Rose Quartz

I lose you every morning
when I open my eyes.

My memory awakens.
I remember you are gone.

I have reclaimed you
through my words.
Brought you to life.
Birthed poems from a place
of loss and healing.

A rose quartz tucked in my left palm
warms, the longer I hold it.
I press the crystal between my breasts,
the rise and fall of my chest
finds its rhythm.

I place my right hand
over my left. Breathe.

Good Morning, Sunshine

Soft pink tones
warm me awake.
My mother extends
a good morning hug
brought to me
by sunrise.

Sky lifts, daylight comes.
She's dressed in magenta, fuchsia
creamy carnation with
sheer soft rose lipstick.

I later sit by the window
in a wicker rocker she once sat in
watch the sun brighten,
a calm wrap around me.
I hear my mother's words

Everything will be ok.

Acknowledgements

Gratitude to the publishing team at Quillkeepers Press for saying "yes" to my manuscript.

Special thanks to the editors, Dylan Webster and Stephanie Lamb for your guidance, inspiration, and graciousness.

Thank you to the Saskatoon Public Library, 2021-2022 Writer in Residence, Di Brandt, for your insightful comments and suggestions to several of my poems. Thank you to Katherine Lawrence, Writer in Residence, Saskatchewan Writers Guild Residency Program at St. Peter's in November 2022. Your guidance and encouragement brought many of these poems to fruition.

To my Sisters' Ink writing group: Your ongoing support, encouragement and love have been a constant in my life for over twenty years. Thank you, Belinda Betker, Dianne Miller, Katherine Lawrence, the late Cindy Clarke, and the late Carla Roppel. I am honored to have worked with such talented women writers!

I am grateful for family and friends who supported Preston's care at home in his last months.

Much love for his team: his wife Harmonie, my daughter Lianna, son-in-law Andre, Preston's best friends, David Arthur, Derek Fiddler, Daniel Toth and Harmonie's sister, Loretta King. Thank you for all the love from the extended King family. To my husband Perry, as we journey through life together, I love you.

About the Author

Lori's mantra is to Experience Connection. She is a poet with heart; her work is soul-centered. Lori Ulrich is a retired teacher who lives on a farm with her husband, close to Saskatoon, Saskatchewan. She writes of family, relationships, and her home prairie landscapes. Lori's stories are published in *Chicken Soup for the Caregiver's Soul*, and *Through My Eyes: 74 True Stories of Survival, Strength and the Power of Believing*. Her poetry has appeared in several magazines and anthologies, including Quillkeepers Press and *Spring Magazine*. She has poems in two chapbooks, along with her writing group, Sisters' Ink, of which she's been a member for over twenty years. She is also a member of the Saskatchewan Writer's Guild. *Turning the Corner* (Quillkeepers Press) is Lori's debut poetry collection.

www.ingramcontent.com/pod-product-compliance
Lightning Source LLC
Chambersburg PA
CBHW060347130626
46553CB00003B/1116

* 9 7 9 8 9 8 6 8 3 8 9 9 1 *